FANDOM FEVER

HARRY STYLES'S
HARRIES

BY VIRGINIA LOH-HAGAN

45th Parallel Press

Published in the United States of America by
Cherry Lake Publishing Group
Ann Arbor, Michigan
www.cherrylakepublishing.com

Reading Adviser: Beth Walker Gambro, MS, Ed., Reading Consultant, Yorkville, IL
Content Adviser: Chloe Mondloch
Book Designer: Joseph Hatch

Photo Credits: © PA Images/Alamy Stock Photo, cover, title page; © Debby Wong/Shutterstock, 4; © Featureflash Photo Agency/Shutterstock, 7; © Mr Pics/Shutterstock, 8; © lev radin/Shutterstock, 11; © Featureflash Photo Agency/Shutterstock, 12; © ECO LENS/Shutterstock, 13; © Michael715/Shutterstock, 14; © lev radin/Shutterstock, 17; Hullian111, CC BY-SA 4.0 via Wikimedia Commons, 19; © Debby Wong/Shutterstock, 21; © lev radin/Shutterstock, 22; © WENN Rights Ltd/Alamy Stock Photo, 25; Raph_PH, CC BY 2.0 via Wikimedia Commons, 26; © Mr Pics/Shutterstock, 29; © Mr Pics/Alamy Stock Photo, 29

Copyright © 2025 by Cherry Lake Publishing Group

All rights reserved. No part of this book may be reproduced or utilized in any form or by any means without written permission from the publisher.

45th Parallel Press is an imprint of Cherry Lake Publishing Group.

Library of Congress Cataloging-in-Publication Data

Names: Loh-Hagan, Virginia, author.
Title: Harry Styles's Harries / Virginia Loh-Hagan.
Description: Ann Arbor : 45th Parallel Press, 2024. | Series: Fandom fever | Audience: Grades 4-6 | Summary: "Harry Styles's Harries provides an inside look at the powerful fandom of Harry Styles. Readers will get hooked on this hi-lo title, covering facts about and insights into the group of fans who aren't afraid to make their support of this heartthrob known"— Provided by publisher.
Identifiers: LCCN 2024009451 | ISBN 9781668947463 (hardcover) | ISBN 9781668948859 (paperback) | ISBN 9781668950371 (ebook) | ISBN 9781668954935 (pdf)
Subjects: LCSH: Styles, Harry, 1994—Juvenile literature. | Popular music fans—Juvenile literature.
Classification: LCC ML3930.S89 L65 2024 | DDC 782.42166092—dc23/eng/20240227
LC record available at https://lccn.loc.gov/2024009451

Cherry Lake Publishing Group would like to acknowledge the work of the Partnership for 21st Century Learning, a Network of Battelle for Kids. Please visit Battelle for Kids online for more information.

Note from publisher: Websites change regularly, and their future contents are outside of our control. Supervise children when conducting any recommended online searches for extended learning opportunities.

Printed in the United States of America

Table of Contents

CHAPTER ONE
From Fan Base to Fandom 5

CHAPTER TWO
Fanning Harry Styles 9

CHAPTER THREE
Living That Fan Life 15

CHAPTER FOUR
The Power of Fandom 20

CHAPTER FIVE
Insider Information 24

Glossary 32
Learn More 32
Index 32

Dr. Virginia Loh-Hagan is an author and educator. She is currently the Director of the Asian Pacific Islander Desi American (APIDA) Center at San Diego State University and the Co-Executive Director of The Asian American Education Project. She lives in San Diego with her very tall husband and very naughty dogs.

Harry ♥

Harry Styles loves his fans. They are called Harries.

CHAPTER ONE

From Fan Base to Fandom

Musicians make music. They perform music. Some become big stars. They become **celebrities**. Celebrities are famous. They have a **fan base**. A fan base is a group of supporters.

Most fans have a casual interest. But some fans are more devoted. They worship their **idols**. Idols are big stars. Devoted fans form **fandoms**. Fandoms are communities. They're networks of fans.

Fandoms of musicians are special groups. They buy the musicians' music. They buy their **merch**. Merch means merchandise. It means stuff that can be sold. Merch includes shirts and posters. Fans follow musicians on tour. They attend their shows. They go on tour with them. They connect with the music. They connect with the messages. They sing their songs. They know all the words.

Fandoms are a powerful force. They can influence music. They use the internet. The internet gives fans information about their idols. It gives them more access to their idols. It also gives them more access to other fans.

Fans build relationships with each other. They share their knowledge. They share their passion. They build connections. They create content. They share content.

Fans make fan art. This is when they draw pictures of their idols. Fans also write stories about their idols. This is called **fan fiction**. They share their art. They share their stories.

Some celebrities have large fandoms. Their fandoms even have special names. That's a sign of success!

xoxo

Harries are loyal Harry Styles fans. They support him. Some have loved him since he was in the band One Direction.

One Direction was formed as part of a TV show. The show was called *The X Factor*.

CHAPTER TWO

Fanning Harry Styles

Harry Styles was born in 1994. He's an English singer. He started singing in 2010. He was part of a band. The band was called One Direction. One Direction was a best-selling boy group.

Styles became a **solo** singer in 2017. Solo means to perform alone. He is a successful singer. But he might be more famous for his fashion. Styles has style. He's also an actor.

His songs are top hits. His movies are top hits. His outfits are also hits. He's been on many magazine covers. He's known around the world. He's won many awards.

Harries are all ages. They're all genders. They're all races. Styles appeals to different people. His music is personal. Fans relate to his music. They don't feel alone. A fan said, "I look up to Harry because I think his music saves a lot of people." Another fan said, "He makes everyone feel very comfortable with themselves…he is very good at expressing himself."

Harries are from all over the world. There are European Harries. There are American Harries. These 2 fan groups argue. European Harries want him to perform in England more. They think he's in the United States too much. Everybody wants more of Styles. They can't get enough of him.

European Harries chant, "Leave America." They do this at his shows.

SUPER FAN

Ashley Frangipane was born in 1994. She's better known as Halsey. Halsey is a singer. She's also a Harrie. She's collected his merch. She has a pillow with his face. She wears his merch. She gets excited about his tour dates. She wrote, "Harry Styles on tour during my birthday? Yep!" Styles put up posters to promote a new album. Halsey joined other Harries. She was trying to figure out Styles's clues. She wrote, "Harry is doing a thing!" Styles and Halsey were on the cover of *Rolling Stone* magazine. Halsey said she and Styles were "twinning." Twinning refers to twins. It means matching. Halsey went to one of Styles's shows. Styles changed the song words for her. He sang "Kiwi." The words are, "I'm having your baby." Halsey just had a baby. Styles sang instead, "You just had a baby." He pointed at Halsey. Two years later, Halsey's son dressed like Styles. He did this for Halloween. For Harries, Halloween is Harryween.

Many fans write fan fiction. Fan fiction is a kind of story. Fans turn idols into characters. They share the stories. They post them online.

Anna Todd is a Harrie. She's been a fan since his One Direction days. She wrote fan fiction about Styles. Her story is called "After." She wrote a series. The main character is Hardin Scott. Scott is modeled after Styles. The series has 3 books. It became a big hit. It was turned into a movie.

Harries had mixed feelings. Some fans liked the series. Some fans didn't. They thought Scott was a bad guy. They think Styles is a better person. They thought Scott ruined Styles's good name.

Anna Todd published a chapter a day. She did this for a year. She did this online. Then she turned the chapters into books.

Harries dress up. An article said, "It's not just a concert when Harry comes to town. It's an event."

CHAPTER THREE

Living That Fan Life

Harries show up at Harry Styles events. To be a Harrie, make sure to look the part! Do the following:

+ Wear colorful outfits. Wear **statement pieces**. These are things you wear. They are showy. Wear feathers. Wear fringe. Wear tassels. Wear sequins. Wear glitter. Wear pearly necklaces. Wear nail polish with gems. Harries are bold. They like to shine. They like to be sparkly.

+ Wear handmade outfits. Harries sew. They crochet. They make their own clothes. They add designs to clothes. They wear one-of-a-kind outfits.

+ Add H.S. to outfits. H.S. stands for Harry Styles.

+ Study Styles's looks. Copy his style. Recreate what he wore. Add something unique.

Harries have their own culture. To be a Harrie, make sure to act the part! Do the following:

+ Add "-rry" to your words. Harries want to connect all words to Harry. An example is saying "bookrry."

+ Do "the whale." Styles takes a sip of water. He spits it up into the air. Water spills down. It looks like a whale shooting water out of its blowhole.

+ Do a "satellite stomp" or "satellite tippy taps." Styles does a little dance. He makes little foot taps. He does this when he sings "Satellite."

+ Bark when Styles arrives on stage. The first time this happened, Styles laughed and barked back. So it kept happening and became a tradition.

Styles is known for putting on a great show.

Fanatic Fan

In 2012, Styles dated Taylor Swift. Swift is a superstar. She has one of the largest fandoms. Her fandom is called the Swifties. She's known for writing songs about her love life. She and Styles broke up. Many fans believed they wrote songs about each other. Swift wrote many songs. For example, she wrote "Style." She wrote "Wildest Dreams." She wrote "I Knew You Were Trouble." She wrote "Out of the Woods." Styles wrote "Ever Since New York." He wrote "Two Ghosts." He wrote "Perfect." There might have been others. Neither singer admitted anything. Fans tried to figure things out. Swifties got really mad. They attacked Styles. They wrote negative comments. Singer Halsey wrote a song about Styles and Swift. The song was called "The Haylor Song." It combined their names.

Not all fan behavior is good. Some fans can be **toxic**. Toxic means harmful. To be a Harrie, don't let your passion become poison. Do the following:

+ Respect Styles's privacy. Orero Tarazaga was a toxic fan. He stalked Styles. He broke into his home. He damaged a plant pot. He did other bad things. Styles banned him from getting near him. He banned him from contacting him.

+ Respect Styles's private life. Styles can date whomever he likes. Fans connected him to another One Direction member. They bullied this person's friends and family.

+ Respect Styles's fashion choices. In 2023, Styles shaved his head. Some fans were upset. They posted mean comments.

People have a right to live their lives. Focus on the art more than the artist.

Harries love seeing Harry Styles on tour.

CHAPTER FOUR

The Power of Fandom

Harries are inspired by their idol. They support him. They support his causes. Together, they're a powerful force. They've helped people. They've made social changes.

Styles has promoted love. He has promoted kindness. He has promoted acceptance. He wore a pin on his guitar strap. He did this in 2017. The pin read, "Treat People With Kindness." It's TPWK for short. Styles added the phrase on merch. It's on shirts. It's on hats. It's on a lot of stuff. Fans bought all these things. The money was donated to support many different charities.

This phrase became a hit. Harries adopted it as a **slogan**. Slogans are catchy phrases. Styles saw his fans wearing TPWK merch. He said, "Oh this is a bit of a thing."

Harry Styles is happy his fans have adopted the TPWK slogan.

Fan responses inspired Styles. Styles wrote a song about TPWK. He released posters to introduce the song. The posters read, "Do you know who you are? TPWK." Fans figured it out. Styles also created a special website. The site sent fans positive messages. Styles ended the notes with "TPWK, H."

Harries supported TPWK. They did the "boot scoot" dance at his shows. They did it when Styles sang the TPWK song. Styles talked to his fans. He said, "Look after each other. I'll see you again when the time is right. Treat people with kindness. I love you more than you'll know."

The TPWK message has spread. Harries add "with kindness" to the end of their sentences. This reminds them to be kind. It also honors Styles.

Harry Styles loves Shania Twain. She influences him.

Idol Inspiration

Idols have idols. Harry Styles is inspired by Shania Twain. Twain is known as the "Queen of Country Pop." Styles said Twain influenced him greatly. He said she impacted his "music and fashion." He grew up listening to Twain. His mother often played Twain's songs. His favorite song is "You're Still the One." Twain is grateful for Styles's support. She said, "He's just been so vocal about it. He plays the song live as well. And it's really beautiful. I met him backstage at one of his concerts, actually. And he did my song in the show. So it was really cool." Styles and Twain are friends. They text each other. They sang together as well. They wore matching sparkly outfits. Fans loved it. They know Twain's songs even though they're young. Twain said, "It's the Harries, his age group and even younger. Their moms had my music on...At some point, they know every word by heart."

CHAPTER FIVE

Insider Information

Fans know their idols. They can also spot fake fans. Make sure you do your research. Here are the top 10 things every true Harrie should know about Harry Styles!

1. Styles was in a school play. He played a church mouse. He loved dressing up. He wore tights. He said, "And that was maybe where it all kicked off!"

2. Styles made his first appearance in 2010. He was on *The X Factor*. He sang "Hey Soul Sister." This song is by Train. He also sang "Isn't She Lovely?" This song is by Stevie Wonder.

3. Styles came up with the name One Direction. He said it doesn't have a special meaning. The name just stuck. Before this, he was in another band. The band was called White Eskimo.

The X Factor judges thought there was something special about Harry.

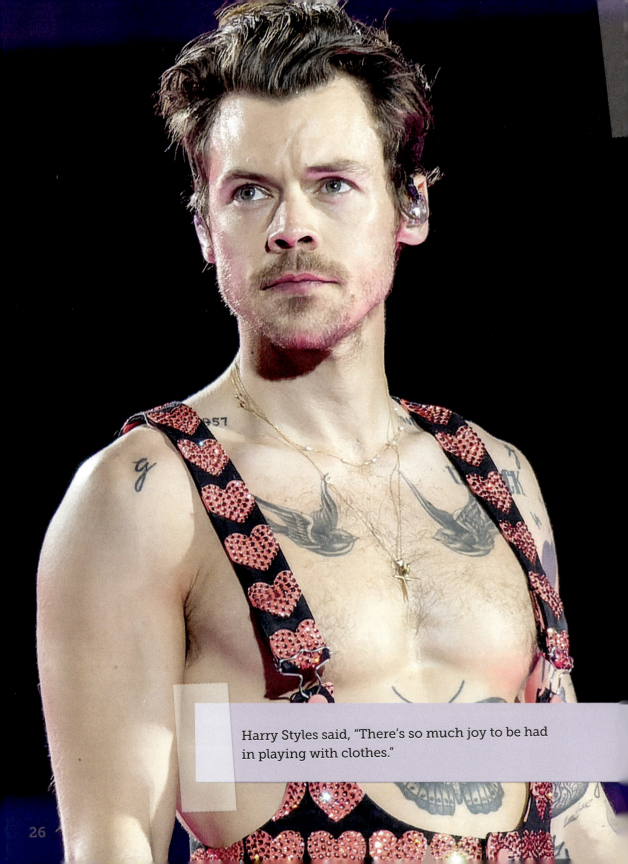

Harry Styles said, "There's so much joy to be had in playing with clothes."

4. Styles worked in a bakery in his hometown of Holmes Chapel, England. His boss said he was the "most polite" worker. Fans travel there and visit the bakery. They also visit other important places in his hometown.

5. Styles has more than 40 tattoos. He got his first tattoo at age 18. One tattoo is a large butterfly. He got another tattoo on TV. He was on a late-night show. He did it as a dare.

6. Styles wrote songs for other artists. He wrote for Ariana Grande and Meghan Trainor.

7. Styles is a fashion **icon**. An icon is a person or thing. An icon is admired in a certain area. Styles owns many suits. Many of them are made by Gucci. He was on the cover of *Vogue* magazine. He wore a dress. He was the first man to appear solo on the cover. He did this in 2020.

8. Styles starred in 4 big movies. These were *Dunkirk*; *Eternals*; *Don't Worry, Darling*; and *My Policeman*.

9. In 2021, Styles launched Pleasing. This is his lifestyle, beauty, and makeup brand. He sells his products around the world.

10. Styles loves reading. He said, "Reading didn't really used to be my thing. I had such a short attention span. But I was dating someone who gave me some books. I felt like I had to read them because she'd think I was a dummy if I didn't read them.'

There's so much more to learn! Make sure to keep up with the latest.

Harry Styles filmed *My Policeman* in 2021.

Fans have their own language. Here are some Harrie words you should know:

+ Eroda: Eroda is a fake island. It was the setting of the "Adore You" music video. Eroda is "adore" spelled backwards.

+ Harry **Baptisms**: Baptisms are religious ceremonies involving water. A person who is baptized becomes part of a church or religious community. Harries want to be baptized by Harry. This marks them as official fans. Styles often throws water into the crowds. He does this at his shows. He opens a TPWK merch water bottle. He runs to the edge of the stage. He throws the water onto fans. Fans try to get splashed.

+ harryflorals: This social media account is on Instagram. It's the top fan account for Styles. It shares updates.

+ Satellite Stompers: Harries invented this term. "Satellite" is one of Styles's songs. Stompers are shoes. Styles wears these shoes when performing the song. He does a little dance. The shoes were designed by Adidas and Gucci.

+ Solo Harries: Solo Harries love Styles. They support only him. They don't support other One Direction band members.

Styles's biggest fan base is teen girls. He said, "How can you say young girls don't get it? They're our future. Our future doctors, lawyers, mothers, presidents. They kind of keep the world going. Teenage-girl fans—they don't lie. If they like you, they're there. They don't act 'too cool.' They like you. And they tell you. Which is sick."

There are all types of Harries. Harries are all around the world. Start your own fan club!

- Promote your fan club.
- Host a meeting.
- Collect a list of names.
- Have fun!
- Plan events.

Harry Styles is an icon in many ways.

GLOSSARY

baptisms (BAP-tih-zuhmz) Christian ceremonies that use water to symbolize rebirth and purification

celebrities (suh-LEH-bruh-teez) well-known or famous people

fan base (FAN BAYSS) group of fans for a particular sport, musical group, or celebrity

fandom (FAN-duhm) subculture, community, or network of fans who share a common interest

fan fiction (FAN FIK-shuhn) stories written by fans featuring their favorite idols and often posted on the internet

icon (IYE-kaan) a person or thing widely admired in a particular area

idols (EYE-duhlz) people who are greatly admired and loved by others

merch (MURCH) short for merchandise, which includes posters, shirts, and other items

slogans (SLOH-gunz) catchy phrases or taglines representing a brand or message

solo (SOH-loh) performing alone, rather than part of a group

statement pieces (STAYT-muhnt PEE-suhz) clothing or accessories that stand out or draw attention

toxic (TAHK-sik) harmful

LEARN MORE

Anderson, Kirsten. *Who Is Harry Styles?* New York, NY: Penguin Workshop, 2023.

Be More Harry Styles: Authentic advice on subverting expectations and embracing kindness. London, England: DK, 2022.

McLaren, Charlotte. *The Book of Harry: A Celebration of Harry Styles.* New York, NY: HarperCollins, 2022.

Schwartz, Heather E. *Harry Styles: Chart-Topping Musician and Style Icon.* Minneapolis, MN: Lerner Publications, 2023.

INDEX

acting, 28–29

concerts, 10–11, 12, 13, 16–17, 19, 22, 23, 30
culture, 15–16, 20–22, 30

dances, 16, 22, 30

famous fans, 12, 18, 23
fandoms, 5–6, 18, 31
fan fiction, 6, 13
fashion
　of Harries, 12, 14, 15
　of Harry Styles, 4, 9, 11, 12, 15, 19, 23, 26

Halsey, 12, 18

imitation, 12, 15, 16, 20

kindness and love, 20–22

merchandise, 5, 20, 28

One Direction, 8, 9, 24

romantic relationships, 18, 19, 28

slogans, 20–22
songwriting, 18, 22, 27

Styles, Harry
　biography and personal life, 9, 18, 19, 24, 27–28
　photos, 4, 7, 8, 11, 17, 21, 25, 26, 29, 31
　talents, 9, 10, 17, 20, 24, 27–28
Swift, Taylor, 18

Todd, Anna, 13
toxic behavior, 19
Twain, Shania, 22, 23

vocabulary, 20–22, 30

The X Factor (television program), 8, 24, 25

32